GOODBYE VIENNA

The story of Gertrude Wertheim as written and illustrated by herself and the recolle
Julian she looked after when she came to England on the Kindertransport in 1938.

In deep gratitude
to the people and Parliament
of the United Kingdom
for saving the lives of
10,000 Jewish and other children
who fled to this country
from Nazi persecution
on the Kindertransport
1938 - 1939

Parliament plaque on the wall in the Palace of Westminster presented by the Association of Jewish Refugees on June 14th 1999

"Whosoever rescues a single soul is credited as though they had saved the whole world"   Talmud

CONTENTS

Gertie Wertheim

Vienna 1938

Aged 15

Preface

In 1938 Gertie Wertheim was just one of 10,000 children under the age of 17 to come to England via what later became known as the Kindertransport. Each and every one of these children had their own stories to tell about their life- changing journey. What was it then that made Gertie's story so particularly special?

Shortly after arriving in England she wrote of her experiences during this period in the form of a short Booklet illustrated by lovely pen and watercolour drawings. These very special drawings have fortunately survived intact and given us a rare glimpse of the events of this period in our history. She entitled her Booklet "My Adventures" by me and it has been reproduced in this Book.

For many decades the Booklet lay untouched in the darkness of a drawer. On the odd occasion when it was looked at it invited many interesting and unanswered questions. Latterly many of these queries have now been resolved, often in the most unlikely and unexpected ways; consequently there is now a story surrounding the Booklet which is now revealed within this Book. Essentially this is a book about a book.

Gertie was just 15 when she arrived at Harwich from Vienna in December 1938. She went to live with the Andrew's Family in Ruislip, Middlesex, where she spent less than a year looking after their five year-old son called Julian. Her time with Julian forms a key part of her Booklet. After more than sixty years, remarkably, Julian was found thanks largely to the powers of the Internet. His recollections of Gertie provided a whole new dimension to the Booklet and are described by him within these pages.

In 1941 Gertie married an Englishman and they had two children. Tragically, she fell victim to the Polio Epidemic of 1951 and died at just 27 years of age.

Accordingly we were unable to talk to her about the events described in her Booklet. Over the years however we have managed to piece together this supporting story which is the result of the combined efforts of many people.

 For those of us involved in the story of Gertie it has been a very satisfying experience and a privilege to be able to record the sequence of events surrounding Gertie's adventures. It is intended to be primarily for the benefit of her descendents but will undoubtedly have wider appeal.

What follows ensures that she will never be forgotten.

Chris and Rod Wilshaw 2015

GRUND NUMMER	0	1	2	8	1	0	2	8

Geburts-Zeugnis.

dem Unterzeichneten wird hiemit bestätigt, daß laut Geburts-Protokolles der israelitischen Kultusgemeinde in Wien, 1923 Reihezahl 1562

Gertrud Wertheim

am 13. Juli 1923 dreizehnten Juli Eintausend neun hundert drei u. zwanzig

als ehelicher Tochter des Miksa Wertheim und der Margit geb. Kohn

in Wien geboren wurde.

Wien, am 30. Juli 1923

MATRIKELAMT DER ISRAELITISCHEN KULTUSGEMEINDE IN WIEN.

[illegible]

beeideter Matrikelführer.

Viennese Origins

Gertrude (Gertie) Wertheim was born in Vienna on July 13th 1923. Her parents were Miksa (Max) and Margit (Grete) nee Kohn. Her birth was registered in the Jewish Community. She had an elder sister, Edith (Ditta), who was born in 1917. They lived in the Jewish Quarter at 1/20 Raffaelgasse Vienna 20 but were non-practising Jews. During the Great War Max served in the Austrian army in Yugoslavia. He owned a shoe shop and was comfortably off with a maid. In the adjoining flat lived Kathe (Kitty) Katscher who was her best friend who also came to England and remained a life -long friend.

Gertie and Ditta

Max and Grete

Gertie and her sister Ditta

Gertie and Kitty

Gertie showed a considerable aptitude for needlework and applied arts. She may have attended the famous Gewerbeschule. Her artistic skills are evident in her Booklet and she put these skills to good practice later in her life.

In the early 1930s anti-Semitism began to spread in Vienna. After Hitler invaded Austria in March 1938 the situation worsened markedly, culminating in the terrible events during the night of Nov 9/10 which became known as Kristallnacht "the Night of the Broken Glass". From then on Jews in Vienna feared for their lives.

Along with many others, the Wertheims took prompt action and on Nov 14th the Home Office in London received a visa application for Gertie to come to England.

There were two main reasons why this could not be immediately granted. Firstly, there was no formal extradition treaty between Britain and Austria. Secondly, and more serious, the recently formed Greater Reich would not consent to a mass exodus of people from Austria. These two apparently insurmountable problems were remarkably overcome. Even more remarkable was the speed at which it happened.

Following the combined lobbying of a number of organisations, including notably the Quakers, the British Government agreed to speed up the immigration process and Agencies promised to find suitable foster parents. Simultaneously, a remarkable Dutch lady called Gertruida Wijsmuller-Meijer, persevered against all the odds and managed to persuade Adolf Eichmann to allow children to leave Vienna by train for England.

The Kindertransport

The first train out of Vienna was on Dec 10th exactly one month after Kristallnacht. Gertie was on the second train which left Vienna's Westbahnhof a week later on Sunday Dec 17th. The children aged between 3 and 17 were allowed to take a small sealed suitcase containing no valuables and no more than 10 marks in money. Identification was by a card with a number written on it and hung around the neck. Gertie was number 64. Parents were not allowed on the platform and had to stand behind barriers to prevent any public display of emotion. The train left early in the evening to reduce any adverse publicity. Soldiers patrolled the corridors. The train was crowded with around 150 children all under the age of 17. Some adults accompanied them but they were under strict orders not to abscond in England with the threat of stopping future trains.

 The journey through Austria and across Germany was slow. Eventually they crossed the Dutch border to their great relief. Dutch ladies in white aprons gave out hot chocolate drinks and fed them dumplings to alleviate the hunger and thirst. After travelling through the night they eventually arrived at the Hook of Holland late the following day in time to take the night boat to Harwich. It must have been with some relief that they boarded the SS Prague and set sail for England.

SS Prague

They arrived in Harwich at 5.30 am on the morning of Tuesday Dec 20th. Her visa was stamped and she proceeded on to a transit camp to begin the next stage of her adventures.

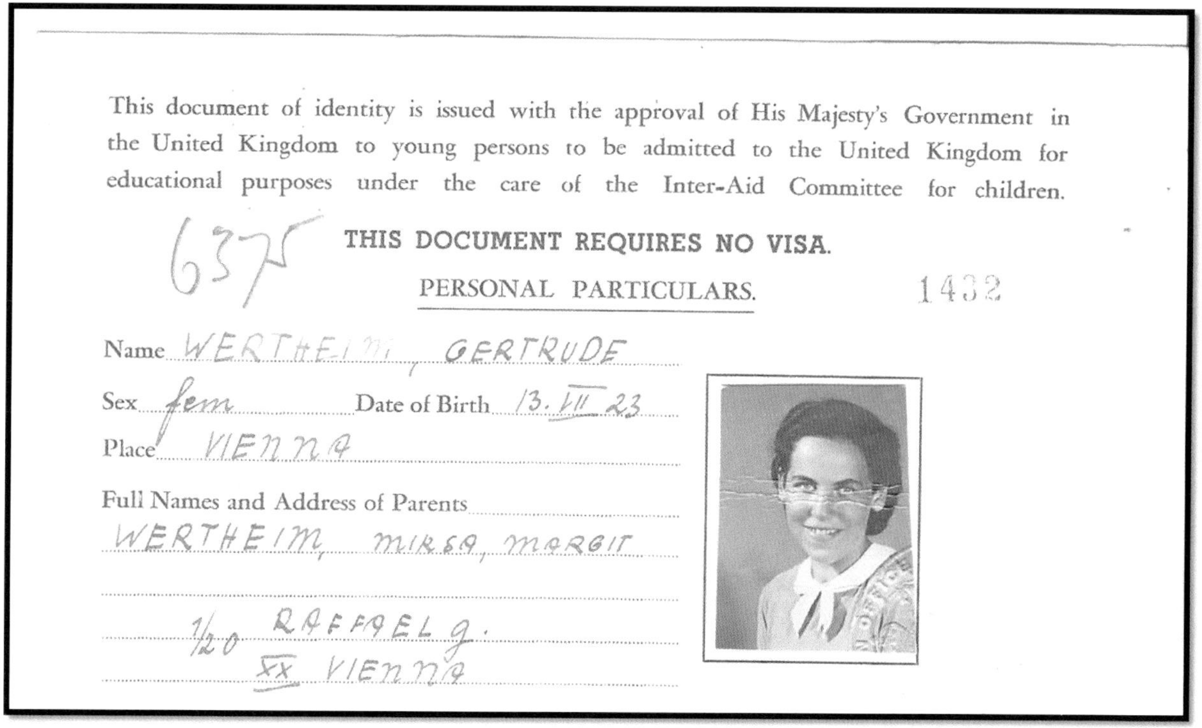

This document of identity is issued with the approval of His Majesty's Government in the United Kingdom to young persons to be admitted to the United Kingdom for educational purposes under the care of the Inter-Aid Committee for children.

6375

THIS DOCUMENT REQUIRES NO VISA.

PERSONAL PARTICULARS.

1432

Name WERTHEIM, GERTRUDE

Sex fem.   Date of Birth 13. VII 23

Place VIENNA

Full Names and Address of Parents

WERTHEIM, MIKSA, MARGIT

1/20 RAFFAEL g.
XX VIENNA

So it was that Gertie, a fifteen year old girl, mature for her years, began her new life in a strange country, where they spoke a foreign language and not knowing anyone. She did not know what lay ahead but compared with many others things were to turn out better than could have been expected. She describes the next phase of her life in a small Booklet which is beautifully illustrated and represents a rare record of life during these troubled times.

It can only be speculated as to exactly when Gertie produced her Booklet. It is highly likely that within that small suitcase she carried with her were her sketch book and watercolours. She probably began her sketches as a record of her experiences as they happened much like an illustrated diary. Only later when she had obtained sufficient command of the English language would she have converted them into the Booklet. The small drawings nested within the text would have been redrawn from the originals whilst the full page drawings are probably the originals. Her Booklet ended abruptly when she left the Andrews Family and started the next phase in her life which soon led to her marriage.

We have reproduced the Booklet here in A5 size and on separate sheets to simulate the original.

REEVES & SONS, LTD., LONDON

Here is a story for you. It is all about my-self — I hope you don't mind! It is my story from the time when I left my home in winter 1938 and came to England. My home was Vienna in Austria and I had a very long way to come. Two days by train from Vienna to Rotterdam as a start. It sounds very nice and quite alright, doesn't it? But I can assure you that it wasn't. You see, I was a-mongst one of the Children's Transports which came from Austria to England very frequently at these times, bringing lots of Refugee-Children over here. There were many children and not very many com-partments in the train so that we were rather crowded. In fact we could hardly move.

Each one of us had a square piece of card board with a number on tied round the neck on a piece of string. My own number was 64. This was done because one can remember numbers better, I suppose. I don't think that I shall ever be able to forget mine, anyway. During the whole journey it became a sort of "second name".

Well, we arrived at Rotterdam, there had a night's rest and then came right across the sea to Harwich. Some of us went straight from Harwich to live with English families. Some others — I amongst these — went to Dovercourt Holiday Camp.

I do think that "Holiday Camp" is the name it deserves. It was a holiday I had there!

We spent our days playing about in the snow, doing
exercises and running about as much as we could. ~
When we felt cold there was a large hall with big
blazing fires waiting for us where we could either
read or write letters home or play games ~ every
thing was ideal and lovely with only a few exep~
tions one of which was a full plate of porridge

which was put in
every morning at
was a terrible, aw-
happen because I
too and ~ honestly
a bit. I tried to
of it by giving
but unfortuna~

front of me
8 o'clock. This
full thing to
had to eat it
I didn't like it
get myself out
it to the cat
tely I soon was

found out. — Playing about regularly tired us out so much that we did not even mind having to be in bed and asleep by half past eight. Some times we were in bed even sooner. Then per≈

haps, just before we were going to sleep, we would come to think of our homes, our parents we had left be≈ hind us ... then there would be a sigh sometimes or even a few tears ..... Still ~

I felt really sorry and got quite a shock when one day a wire came for me.

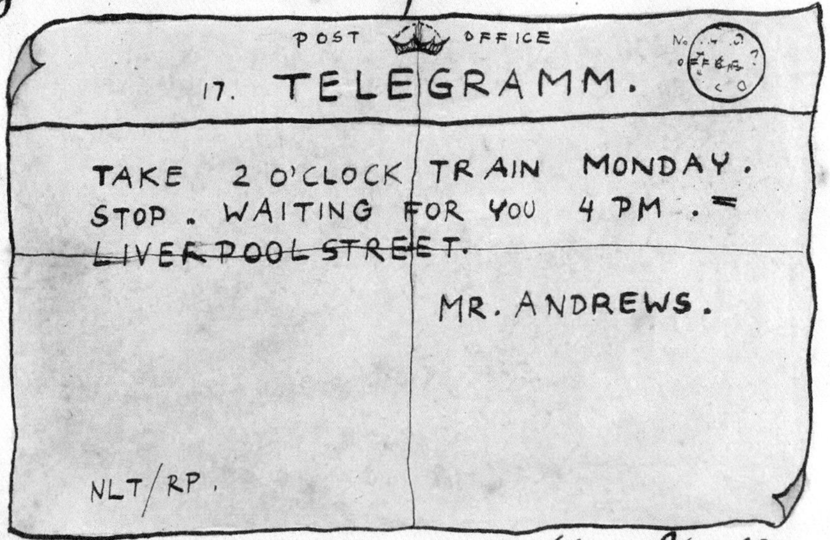
POST OFFICE
17. TELEGRAMM.
TAKE 2 O'CLOCK TRAIN MONDAY.
STOP. WAITING FOR YOU 4 PM. =
LIVERPOOL STREET.
MR. ANDREWS.
NLT/RP.

I was told that this was the family I was to go and stay with. So I said good bye to fun

friends and forgetting, packed my case and went to London. When I arrived at Liverpool street Station I started searching for Mr. Andrews and nearly bumped right into a grim and important looking porter.
After I had apologised in German, not knowing any English, he suddenly started talking to me. English, I guess, anyway I didn't understand a single word. Luckily just then Mr. Andrews came along and saved me from him. He spoke German exellently which was very usefull.

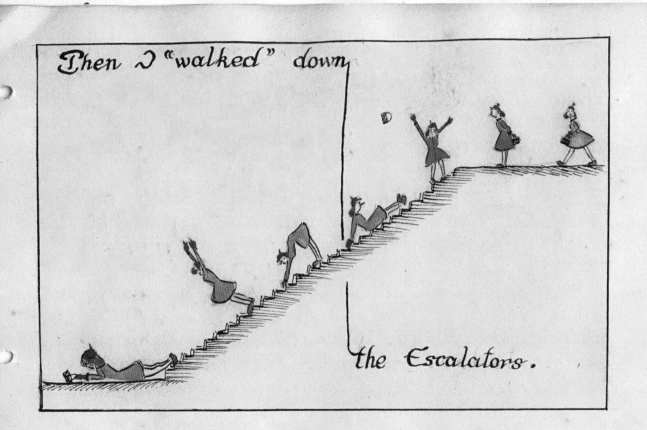

I had never seen any before and — as you see, found it rather a job to walk down on them. After I landed at the bottom we took a train. I had never seen any self-closing doors either, we dont have them in Vienna.

Mr. Andrews took me to some friends of his. His own home was in a small place — in Middlesex and I was to stay with his friends for a fortnight to have a good look at London before I went in the country. I had a good look at it, too! The very kind lovely lady took me to all the different places in a 'bus. Sometimes her husband came, too. They were both very kind to me, tried to make me feel at home and to teach me English. They had two cats ~ but they weren't much good because there was no porridge to be eaten. I spent Christmas with them ~ a very gay, noisy Christmas with a lot of people and burning Christmaspuddings it was, but I did miss my family so dreadfully! The last Christmas I had spent at home had been gay too, but it was a hearty kind of gayness.

On New Years Eve we went to Piccadilly Circus together to see the crowd. All the laughter, cheery faces, smiles and songs it was lovely! Then a more serious time began. Mr. Andrews fetched me in his car and I said good-bye to the kind lady and her husband and went to look after four puppies and a little boy, called Julian. We very soon made friends all six of us and very often went for long walks together. Julian's mother was a tall, slim lady. She too was just as kind to me as her husband. I was very lucky, wasn't I? And above all Julian was a good little boy who scarcely was badtempered. I soon settled down quite happily. To make things better still my mother and sister wrote, that there was at last a possibility of them getting out of Austria. I did all I could for them to get an English visa and a permission to enter this country. Soon after I had received their letter I was able to await my sister on Liverpool-Street station. Mr. A. took me down in the car. It was a mad race

all through London. We were rather late and so Mr. Andrews drove as quick as he could. We actually bumped into a 'bus!
All the trafficlights seemed to turn red

as soon as we got to them and we had to stop at a garage to get some more petrol, too. Then at last we got to the station and rushed unto the platform — only to find that the train was two hours late.

So we wondered around Liverpool street ~ Station for two hours. Then the train came in and my sister climbed out and we were all very happy. My sister ~ her name is Ditta ~ went to live with another English family as a governess. She was looking after a little girl and a little boy.

I had by then picked up some English and I felt very superior to Ditta as she was not able to talk English at all, just like me when I first came. I often found myself correcting her ~ to Mrs. Andrews' amusent.

So spring came into the country, the garden began to show little tiny flowers and the trees started wearing a lovely pale green coat. Just before Easter mother wrote telling us that she was coming in a couple of days. Again we went to the station ～ this time without an accident ～ again the train was in two hours later and again we were very glad. It was lovely to be united again. I learned to appreciate "being together".

Mother stayed with the kind lady I had been staying with when I first arrived in England untill she found a job. Being mother, she simply had to bring us some presents from home, too. One of my presents I rembered was a huge doll with a big bow and chinablue eyes. A silly thing to have sitting on one's lap going home with it in the train, isn't it? But I survived!

Well, mother found a job for herself until she would be able to go to America to join her fiancé. She soon settled down. We saw each other frequently and life began to cease being like a weird strange dream alltogether. There was a beauti-

ful holiday at Newquay with the Andrews —
Julian and I had the fun of our lives ba-
thing in the sea, catching little crabs and
making castles in the sand! There were fre-
quent "going's-out" to shows and dances
with new friends I had gradually acquired. Also I used to dance or practice tap-
dancing in my sparetime.

    After a while I started making
plans for the future. Maybe I could take
up my Arts and Crafts again where I had
had to interrupt them in Vienna? Or maybe I could go to the stage as a dancer?

    We would follow mother to America as
soon as she had settled there . . . .

Then with a shock that left us all numb War started. Mrs. Andrews decided to go to Wales. We packed in a hurry and were off within 48 hours. Mr. Andrews, being an officer in the Territorials joined his regiment and the three of us were driven down to Wales by a friend. I had hardly time to say good-bye to mother and Ditta — it was all one constant long rush.

When we got to the farm in Poly bont,

I found it to be a very small, old fashioned village where everybody stared at you when you wore slacks. It had beautiful surroundings and on my afternoons off I went for long hikes. When Whiskey the dog felt like it, she came, too. Also I took snaps of simply everything — including cows.

Often I took Julian down to the little river or to the beach to float his toyboat or his ducks or his fishes.

Dovercourt

Now and again Gertie's Booklet would be taken from the dark drawer in which it was stored, protected from the sunlight which is why it has survived in such good condition. There were a number of queries which always excited curiosity and which over the years have now been largely resolved, for example, what and where was Dovercourt? One day quite out of the blue this particular mystery was solved.

Around the year 2000 whilst driving to Harwich for a holiday in Holland we quite unexpectedly saw a signpost pointing to Dovercourt. We immediately followed it and discovered that Dovercourt is in fact a township adjoining Harwich. We went straight to the local library to find out what took Gertie here in 1938. It turned out that this small seaside resort was frequented by Londoners during the short summer season and many of them stayed in a Holiday Camp run by Warners. Due to its close proximity to Harwich and also as it was out of season in December, this Camp was an ideal place to house a large number of refugee children (including Gertie)   who were in transit for various reasons.

The accommodation would not have had heating facilities and the winter of 1938/39 was a particularly cold one. Gertie seems to have enjoyed her stay here and describes playing in the snow and the welcoming fire she warmed herself round.She gives the impression of being there longer than the few days she spent. She arrived on Dec 20th and went up to London in time for Christmas with friends of the Andrews. The town's folk of Dovercourt were notably hospitable and treated the children to the cinema and gave them ice cream treats.

Warner Holiday Camp at Dovercourt

The Warner Holiday Camp at Dovercourt (generally referred to as simply Dovercourt camp) was built in 1937. The camp famously provided the setting for the highly acclaimed BBC TV Comedy "Hi-de-Hi "which was first shown in 1980. Filming was carried out in the spring before the holiday makers arrived. Despite regularly handling 11,000 visitors each year, the camp was closed down at the end of the 1990 season and demolished to make way for a new housing development.

Gertie

When Gertie came to England she had been studying applied arts and drawing and was very good at needlework. What other children would have enjoyed wartime blackout curtains heavily covered with embroidered flowers and appliqués of rabbits in their bedroom?!!

Although she only spent less than 12 months with the Andrew's Family, they gave her good start to her new life in this Country. She learnt English very quickly. She advertised to teach German in exchange for

being taught English, which how she met her future young husband, Leslie John Osborne (known as John to members of his family and Les to everyone else). She later taught Les' nephew Douglas.

They were soon to be married in November 1940 at a Registry Office and followed on with a reception in Aunty Rosie's house in Pinner.

Gertie with her Family

Gertie and Les attended the Quaker Meeting House in Rayners Lane, Harrow.

 Gertie, still only 17 years of age and Les was 23. The next year their first child, Christine, was born, to be followed by a son, Martin, in 1946.

Gertie was a lively mother and as children we can remember lovely picnics and walks together through the same woods she had taken Julian earlier. Many happy times were spent in summer on the "beach" at

Ruislip Lido. She loved dancing and was a leading light in establishing the local branch of the League of Health and Beauty which also included the young daughters of Members.

Tragically, in 1951, at the very young age of 27, she was struck down in the Polio Epidemic.

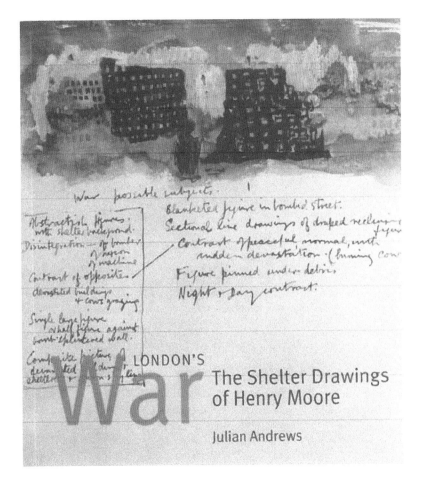

London's

War

The Shelter Drawings of Henry Moore

Julian Andrews

During the Second World War Henry Moore did a series of drawings of Londoners sleeping on the underground station platforms as they escaped the Blitz. Julian wrote the first book describing the drawings in the context of those times in 1940-41.

It was thanks to this book that we were able to locate him.

Finding Julian

We had always wondered what had become of that little boy Julian who played such a key role in her Booklet, albeit for only a short time. Was he still alive? If so, could he be traced?

Remarkably, our daughter managed to track him down using the Internet. It turned out that Julian had been working as an arts envoy for the British Council and through their auspices had published a book about the Shelter Drawings of Henry Moore. Julian was contacted through his publisher and we arranged a meeting.

This turned out to be most rewarding experience imaginable. Julian was able to provide so much background to the descriptions in the Booklet along with photographs.

Finding Julian was like unearthing a lost treasure. We enjoyed many subsequent meetings with him and he brought the Booklet to life through his accounts of the same events which Gertie had recorded in her Booklet. Julian provided wonderfully articulate reminiscences. It was very clear that Gertie had left a very deep impression on him during their brief time together.

During the War Julian had gone to live in Talybont, where he had been evacuated when War was declared. He spent his childhood there, before going up to Cambridge University. When he retired from the British Council he returned to live in his beloved Wales, at Llandebr, close to where he had spent his childhood. We met him there on a few occasions and are deeply grateful for all that he gave us.

Julian died on May 4th 2010. His Obituary was published in the Independent Newspaper.

What follows is an account, by Julian, of the events which lead up to Gertie joining up with the Andrews Family and their time with her. It represents the viewpoint of a person who played a role in providing the opportunity for a refugee like Gertie to come and live in this Country. Julian became an accomplished writer during his career with the British Council and this is evident in the style and content of his writing of this beautifully crafted essay.

Memories of Gertude Wertheim

By

Julian Andrews

This note is being written as a pendant to the short manuscript by Gertrude Wertheim, which her descendants are donating to the collections. Gertie, as she was known, was a 15 year old refugee from Austria who arrived in Britain in December 1938, and on one of the first of the "Kindertransport" trains from Vienna. After a brief spell in a converted holiday camp at Dovercourt, near Harwich, she was taken in by as English family, a Mr. and Mrs. Andrews of Ruislip, Middlesex, who had a 4 year -old son named Julian. Only recently have I learned that it is my own family who are described in her account, from Gertie's daughter and granddaughter, who have managed to trace me. It has been an emotional experience for all of us, to make this personal contact after so many years.

Inevitably my memories are fragmentary, since I was extremely young when she came to us. As far as I can tell she only stayed with us about 10 months, until the outbreak of war divided our family too. At the time I was too young to understand why she had come, or where from, or why she vanished again, but what I do remember is that when the war started everything in my life suddenly altered. So her sudden disappearance was probably just another symptom of those changes. I remember that I missed her, and that my mother often spoke of her, but the image of her faded in my mind, until so recently brought back by her story and drawings, and by the photographs of her which I have found in our old albums. The background was as follows:

My father was Wilfred Francis Andrews, always known as Frank, and he married my mother Josephine Mary Caldwells (Josie), in 1930. I was born on the 11th February 1934. My father worked in a firm of stockbrokers in the City of London, as a specialist in investments, while my mother had done some secretarial training before getting married at the age of only 19. She was extremely talented at drawing and in retrospect it is sad that she never had any training in art or design. Shortly after their marriage they commissioned a new house on an estate being built in Ruislip, which became No 12 Poplar Close, though for reasons unknown to me they called it "The Bear". The house is still there and is a classic example of 1930s design, with a green tiled roof and various art- deco/modernist decorative features. However Gertie never lived in this house, though she would certainly have been taken to see it. It is just round the corner from where we were staying when she was with us.

At some point in 1937/1938 my father moved to another job up in Leeds, Yorkshire, so the Ruislip house was rented out on a contract. During our fairly short stay up in Yorkshire we had a holiday in North Wales, staying at Ty Isaf Farm in Talybont on the coast between Barmouth and Harlech. But presumably the Leeds job did not work out, so sometime in late 1938 we returned to Ruislip. Because their own house was not available my parents rented Crossley House in King Edwards Road, and this must have happened at exactly the time Gertie arrived in England. I assume my parents must have heard the appeal that went out on the BBC home service for families to take in the refugee children, and I assume also the reason she first of all stayed with friends of my parents was that Crossley House was not yet ready, since our furniture had to be retrieved from store. However it seems from her account that she came to us very shortly after Christmas 1938, or in the first days of 1939.

I recall Crossley House as a large building, probably of the 1910 or 1920s period to judge from neighbouring houses visible in the photographs. My mother used to breed pedigree dogs as a hobby, and while Gertie was with us our bull--terrier, Whisky, produced a litter which was exciting for both of us. I also had my little ginger cat, named Marmalade, who is beside Gertie in one of the photos.

The arrival of Gertie must have been a tremendous boost for my mother, who was herself only 28 at the time Not only did Gertie help her with the household chores, and – particularly -- with caring for the five - year-old child, but she was artistic too, having begun an Arts and Crafts course in Vienna. Was it the world-. famous Kunst und Gewerbe Schule, I wonder? Certainly some of the drawings in her little book (left so sadly unfinished) are classic examples of the Art Deco style of the period. They must have loved looking at each other's drawings.

Gertie with puppies and Marmalade

I think of Gertie as a cheerful presence, but cannot claim to have remembered her appearance beyond the reminders of the surviving photographs. But I do remember that she used to take me out for walks. Ruislip was then very much the Metroland made famous later on by John Betjeman in his series of television films. I have memories of a very warm summer, with the sun beating down on hot pavements, bright new brickwork, and sticky asphalt with its strange pungent smell. As we walked the quiet streets we used to listen out for the tinkling bell of the ice-cream man on his large tricycle, with the slogan on the box saying "Stop me and Buy one!" My favourite was the 'sno-frute', a triangular cardboard tube like the shape of the Swiss Toblerone chocolate, containing frozen fruit juice in deep raspberry red, bright orange and other colours. If you licked it too quickly it hurt the sinuses, too slowly and it would melt all over your hands. Gertie would clean mine before we got home. Another favourite walk was to one of the three (or four?) Ruislip railway stations. This station had, in addition to local and (I think) Underground trains, through lines for the fast express trains from Paddington, headed for the West Country. We knew that at certain times particularly noisy, hissing steam locomotives would thunder through, their coaches rattling behind, making me squeal with delight while clinging to Gertie for security.

Another place we went to as a family, at weekends, was an area of woodland close to Ruislip Lido, on a large reservoir. An excellent photograph has survived which I am certain was taken on my fifth birthday, 11th February 1939, showing my mother, father, Gertie and me all in line playing a game of trains. It is clear from the position of my hands that I was the locomotive and they represented the piston rods. That photo seems to me quite symbolic in its feeling of happiness, with the young refugee laughing away, enclosed quite literally in the arms of her new family.

In July1939 we all went down to Cornwall for an idyllic summer holiday, travelling on the Cornish Riviera Express and staying at the Trebarwith Hotel in what was then the small resort of Newquay. We took with us my paternal grandfather, Thomas Andrews, who appears in photographs wearing a suit, waistcoat, and hat and carrying an umbrella City-style in the blazing sun, on the sand and rocks of Towan Beach just below the Hotel, with its natural swimming pool filled twice a day by the tides. It was a blissful time : my father rented small surf boards for Gertie and me , and we adored romping in the strong foaming waves which rolled in from the Atlantic. I remember the incredible feeling of weight and strength in the water as it pushed us up the beach. We both loved the sensation of being picked up and thrown forward with the surf hissing and bubbling inside our ears, when you 'caught' the wave correctly. The experts on their huge boards today get no more pleasure out of it than we did then on our little 'belly-boards '. We made excursions to Crantock and down to Perranporth, where there are photos of Gertie and me on the dunes. In her drawings she has even recalled the white sunhat that I was wearing. Times that have vanished into the mists of memory, surviving only in her pictures and in the photos.

As Gertie mentions, my father was an officer in the Territorial Army, with which he used to go away each summer, in addition to evening and weekend training. He was clearly aware that war was likely to come in the not –too-distant future, and he and my mother must have made plans because he knew he would have to join his regiment on the very first day – which in fact he did. They must have remembered the farm in Wales and got in touch with Mr. And Mrs. Jones to see whether it would be possible to evacuate up there to avoid the threatened bombing of London, which everyone assumed would start at once. So all the furniture went into store once more, the lease on Crossley House was given up, and the three of us - my mother, Gertie and I - set out for Wales.

In due course I was to find a completely new life up there, but for the moment all I could feel was a tremendous sense of loss, something I can still vividly recall, as a real anguish. Everything had gone, our home, my father, our local friends, all my toys including my recently acquired train set, and then Gertie disappeared as well. I had no idea of why any of this had happened or why there were no sweets, no ice-creams, no bananas. All I knew was that people shrugged their shoulders and talked about a mythical time called "before –the – war" which I began, more and more, to associate with warmth and happiness, in which Gertie had been an intimate part,. I missed her, but I was of course still extremely young, and when my mother talked of her (as she often did) I found that she, too, was becoming a part of that myth.

Only now, sixty-nine years later, have I learned the latter part of her story , which brought her the happiness of a husband and children of her own, before her tragically early death. I can only hope that she always remembered her time with my family as a good moment in a fractured life. The inconveniences which we complained about during the war were nothing compared to what she – and millions like her – had to endure. Her cheerfulness must have done so much to help us all.

Gertie and Julian

Julian Andrews 2007

Safe Keeping

The time eventually came to decide on the future of the Booklet. Should it be passed down within Gertie's family or some suitable alternative place?

The Imperial War Museum at Duxford is the custodian of historical material relating to the Holocaust and we donated the Booklet to its archives in 2007. Julian wrote his account to accompany it and they are stored together in the archive. For reference on the Internet search "Miss Gertrude Wertheim". It is now in safe hands and has already benefitted from being rebound and restored.

Stephen Walton Archivist at the Museum informed us:

"The booklet came back from the conservators the other day, and I think that they have done a very good job with it – it essentially looks exactly as before, except that the pages are now properly bound rather than held together by metal rings, making the item much sturdier. I am struck once again by the quality of the pictures and the freshness of the colours, as though the booklet had been created a few weeks ago."

Before it was sent we obtained some very fine facsimiles, made by two friends Joan and Gerald Lee for all the members of the Family.

The very fact that the Museum accepted the Booklet is testimony to its significance and we hope that future generations may benefit in some way from it.

Epilogue

Initially, what began solely as a Booklet has now over a period of time developed into a story about itself. Gertie entitled the Booklet "My Adventures" and indeed for her they were. That is not to say that the Kindertransport was nothing less than heart rending. Note her very poignant reference to the crying of the younger children at Dovercourt who were missing their parents. In her case she did not suffer from loosing family in the Holocaust as so many of her contemporaries did. Also, what spirited girl of 15 years would not be excited at the prospect of visiting a new country with all its attributes? She was very fortunate in being taken in by the Andrews Family who made a home for her. She was obviously a great asset to them and was much adored by Julian.

We have been very fortunate to have found Julian and his "Memories of Gertie" have filled in a big gap in our own memories of her.

Originally Gertie had intended to move on to the USA to follow her mother and pursue a career in dancing; however she met her husband to be and went on to start a family of her own. She was very vivacious and spread happiness around her.

Sadly, her life was cut short by a sudden illness when she was in her prime at a mere 27 years of age, leaving behind a husband and two very young children.

However, through her Booklet and all the associated experiences it has allowed us to share, her memory lives on.

Thank you Gertie!

Gertie Osborne

Ruislip 1951

Aged 27

Acknowledgements

We could not have compiled this account without the help of many lovely people who have given us their time and efforts. Finding Julian was the most uplifting experience and this was due to the initiative of our daughter. Julian proved to be a godsend; not only did he share with us the events surrounding Gertie during those distant days, but he had a special way of expressing them. We could never have parted with the Booklet had we not had an acceptable replacement. Our friends Gerald and Joan Lee made perfect facsimiles on similar Reeves paper used in the original. It is copies originally made by them which we have reproduced here. Lillian Levy of World Jewish Relief Archive released original material which is shown here and was hitherto unknown to us. Stephen Walton of the Imperial War Museum was instrumental in finding a permanent home for this valuable item. The final impetus for publishing this work came from Andrew Gill of the University of the Third Age who gave us his valuable encouragement and expertise.

Printed in Great Britain
by Amazon